Thin Ice

Written by Anne Curtis

Illustrated by Chris Corner

 Collins

We sailed to the Antarctic ...
like Captain Scott in 1901.

2

3

We were exploring when
a blizzard started.
I lost my friends.

I looked for shelter.

Is this Hut Point
where Scott lived?

Scott's diaries were inside.
I read about his
journey, and
what he did in
the Antarctic.

Scott and his crew had made
notes on the animals and
weather to send back home.
Nothing had changed here
for thousands of years.

But how everything is changing.
One day we might drill for oil here.
And everything Scott found will
be lost.

Now I understand why we must protect the Antarctic.

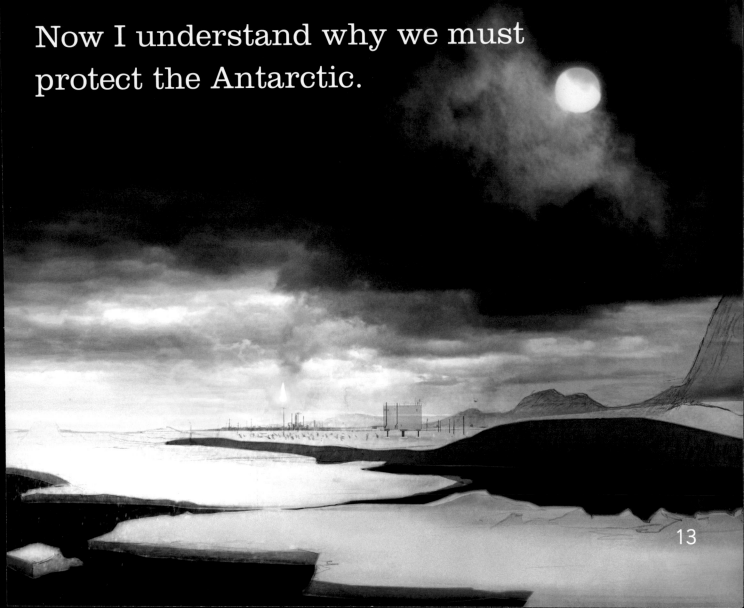

A journey to Antarctica

Ideas for reading

Written by Gillian Howell
Primary Literacy Consultant

Learning objectives: *(reading objectives correspond with Yellow band; all other objectives correspond with Diamond band)* use phonics to read unknown words; understand underlying themes, causes and points of view; recognise rhetorical devices used to argue, persuade, mislead and sway the reader; use a range of oral techniques to present persuasive arguments; select words and language drawing on their knowledge of literary features and formal writing

Curriculum links: History: What can we learn about recent history by studying the life of a famous person?; Geography: Weather around the world

High frequency words: we, to, the, like, in, were, when, a, I, my, for, is, this, where, lived, about, his, and, what, he, did, made, on, back, home, had, here, of, but, now, one, day, will, be, must

Interest words: Antarctic, blizzard, shelter, diaries, thousands, drill, protect

Resources: globe or world map, paper, pens, internet

Word count: 101

Getting started

- Read the title together and look at the cover illustration. Ask the children what impression the image gives them of the content of the book, e.g. *Where in the world has conditions like this? What would it be like to be there?*

- Ask the children to turn to the back cover. Read the blurb together and discuss what the children already know about the Antarctic. Use a globe or world map to point it out.

- Ask the children what they know about Captain Scott. If needed, explain that he was an explorer in Antarctica in the early twentieth century. Discuss the role of an explorer and what it would be like to be one.

Reading and responding

- Ask the children to read the book quietly. Listen to the children as they read and prompt as necessary. Remind the children to use their knowledge of sounds to work out new or difficult vocabulary.